Okehan
People

Mike and Hilary Wreford

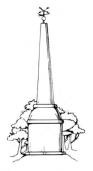

OBELISK PUBLICATIONS

Also by the Authors
Okehampton Collection
Okehampton Collection II
Okehampton Collection III

Other Dartmoor Titles
Diary of a Dartmoor Walker, *Chips Barber*
Diary of a Devonshire Walker, *Chips Barber*
The Great Little Dartmoor Book, *Chips Barber*
The Great Little Chagford Book, *Chips Barber*
Walks in the Chagford Countryside, *Terry Bound*
The Great Walks of Dartmoor, *Terry Bound*
The A to Z of Dartmoor Tors, *Terry Bound*
Ten Family Walks on Dartmoor, *Sally and Chips Barber*
Six Short Pub Walks on Dartmoor, *Sally and Chips Barber*
Widecombe – A Visitor's Guide, *Chips Barber*
Cranmere Pool – The First Dartmoor Letterbox, *Chips Barber*
Circular Walks on Eastern Dartmoor, *Liz Jones*
Walks in the Shadow of Dartmoor, *Denis McCallum*
Walks in Tamar and Tavy Country, *Denis McCallum*
Dark and Dastardly Dartmoor, *Sally and Chips Barber*
Weird and Wonderful Dartmoor, *Sally and Chips Barber*
The Templer Way, *Derek Beavis*
Railways on and around Dartmoor, *Chips Barber*
Princetown of Yesteryear I, *Chips Barber*
Princetown of Yesteryear II, *Chips Barber*

We have over 150 Devon-based titles –
for a list of current books please write to us at:
2 Church Hill, Pinhoe, Exeter, EX4 9ER
telephone (01392) 468556

Acknowledgements
Special thanks to Barrie Hall of Okehampton for pictures on page 6, 18 (top), 23 (bottom) and 25 (top). Also to the *Express & Echo* for reproduction of the 'Stils' cartoons, the *Okehampton Times,* the *Western Times,* Joan Pauley, Bob Gale, Cynthia Sheppard, Sandy Powell, Ted Cann, Ann Bassett, Tom Endacott, Beatrice Fullwood, Colin Lennox-Jones, Pam Norris, Fred Barlow B.E.M. and Vera Kingdon. Also Cinnabar Photography of Okehampton for the modern Rugby Club picture. The Town Crest is reproduced by kind permission of Okehampton Town Council.

First published in 1998 by
Obelisk Publications, 2 Church Hill, Pinhoe, Exeter, Devon
Designed by Chips and Sally Barber
Typeset by Sally Barber
Printed in Great Britain by
Greenhill Press, Newton Abbot, Devon

Okehampton People

'Okehampton People', like folks anywhere else, come in all shapes and sizes. This little book features faces old and new, young and old, past and present. If you have any lasting links with the town then you are bound to know somebody included within these pages. When we set out on this book we had no idea just how many familiar faces we would encounter, but also how many not so well known to us. We talked to townsfolk and were amused and amazed by their reactions to the photos. "There's old what's 'is name!" was a common comment but what was his name, her name? We did our best to get names right but when you are given three different names for one person what do you do? Therefore, rather than play safe we have given names where possible, and sincerely hope that we don't cause any mild offence if we are off the mark with one or two of the thousand or so faces which peer from these pages.

This mini-archive of people pictures will be a lasting social record of times past, and we have included some present-day pictures (at the time of writing!) to show that today's activities will become yesterday's memories. When we compiled this collection we tried to get people in a variety of activities from civic duties to sports teams. We hope you will enjoy the nostalgia and the personal memories which will be rekindled through these pages. They show that Okehampton, a small but lively Dartmoor borderland town, has a sense of community and is a wonderful place in which to live.

We start with a proud moment for the Baptist Sunday School… The Sunday Schools in the town in 1954 were very strong and the Baptist was no exception. These proud children were recipients of the N.S.S.U. Scripture Examination Cup in 1954. This was an examination for Sunday Schools of all denominations within the Exeter Area and Okehampton Baptist Sunday School, although one of the smallest Schools entered within the Exeter District, won the cup by achieving the highest average result, the presentation being made in the Mint Methodist Church in Exeter.

In these days of equal opportunity, it is perhaps interesting to note that there was only one boy amongst the successful team. Perhaps the team was helped by the fact that the Minister's three daughters were included. (Left to Right) Back Row: Jenny Pedrick, Pam Ware, Ann Swaddling. Middle Row: Christopher Parsons, Audrey Brown, Carol Bebb, Pam Hammett. Front Row: Pam Brown, Christine Brown, Rev. G. Hedley Brown, Janice Watkins, Janet Ware.

This photograph of the 1938 St James' Church Choir shows the strength of the choir at that time with over 30 choristers. The Parish Church Choir was equally supported and there was great friendly rivalry between them, with the two choirs joining forces at the parish church just twice a year – at Christmas and Easter. These were the days of the seaside outings and all the Sunday Schools in the town, with parents and choirs, could enjoy a day's return trip by a specially chartered train to such places as Exmouth, Teignmouth or Paignton! The choristers went free. In the evening of the day, as the travellers returned to Okehampton, they would be met by the Okehampton Excelsior Band, under the popular conductor James (Jimmy) Gale, at the railway station and march down Station Road, singing as they proudly marched behind the band. One improvised rendition was: "God save the Engineer for taking us away, God save the Engineer for bringing us home safe again."

A large number of this choir were soon to join the Forces and serve their King and Country.

One interesting story is that the Rev. Lamp met and fell in love with a young lady called Miss Post. Some of the younger children at the time would refer to them as the "Lamp-posts" – but all in good fun! Sally Holmes had, for many years, played the piano at the Okehampton Picture Palace in Market Street in the days of the silent films.

Back Row: Derek Stubbs, Reg Webber, Fred Barlow, Jack Wykes, Eric Chowings, Jack Bolt. 3rd Row: Betty Wykes, Ivy Wykes, Les Bolt, Tom Pedrick, Arthur Vanstone, Jack Hardar, Cyril Westlake, Cecil Bevan, Roy Heale, Peggy Bolt, Phyllis Palmer, Evelyn Glover. 2nd Row: Ethel West, Ruth Down, Betty Bolt, Dorothy Williams, John Palmer, Ron Gratton, Stan Horne. Front Row: Ivy Horne, Peggy Woolland, Georgina Woolland, Joyce Tucker, Rev. Lamp, Rev. Franklin, James Gale, Sally Holmes, Mary Hucker, Phil Smith.

The Okehampton Parish Church First Rover Scout Group was formed at the instigation of Roy Lobb. This 1940 photograph was taken outside the old scout hut in Market Street, which is now the site of the church hall. All the scouts and the two scoutmasters volunteered for the Forces and, except for one who failed on medical grounds, were soon in uniform. Roy Lobb returned to Okehampton after the war, where he continued his employment as manager of Hepworths, and his reputation and diligence gained the branch many customers. He was also able to follow the family tradition of contributing a great deal of selfless energy to the Scout movement. It also reflects great credit that two members, namely Walter Passmore, with the M.B.E., and Fred Barlow, B.E.M., were to be decorated in later life. Fred, of course, was a founder member of the Dartmoor Rescue Group, which was founded in 1968, following the deaths of two officer cadets from Kenya on Dartmoor in 1967. This has developed, with sections at Okehampton, Tavistock, Ashburton and Plymouth, with members giving much time and effort, often in atrocious conditions, to help other people in distress.

Back Row: Bill Willoughby, Reggie Webber, Jack Bolt, R. Beaumont, Fred Barlow, Walter Passmore, J. Beaumont, Les Bolt. Seated: Ivor Davis (Scoutmaster), Roy Lobb (Group School Leader), Mr Simmons (County Commissioner), L. Watson (Rover Scout Leader), Rev. Pickering (Scout Padre).

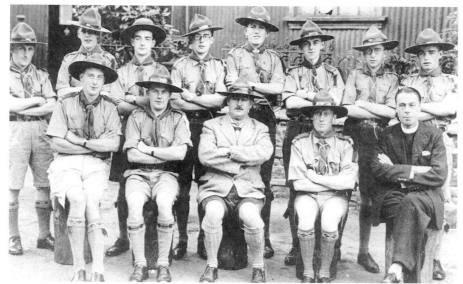

There was great excitement amongst the Scouts as, on 27 May, 1961, the Mayor of Oke–hampton, Mr. W. J. Passmore, officially opened the new Headquarters of the 1st Okehampton Group of Boy Scouts. Pictured along with Mr. Passmore are dignitaries Roy Lobb, Clem White, Sam Wooldridge, Irene Wooldridge, Rev. Radford, Mrs Vick, Mr Rudd, Jack Acton, Bill Brock, Bill Cornish and the Mayoress, Daisy Passmore. The Scout contingent were represented by Bill Bourne, Terry Bevan, John Hubber, Mervyn Westlake, Robert Letchford, Bill Lodge, Nigel Beer, Michael Ellis, Derek Yeo, John Hawkins, Robert Ellis, Richard Glover, Clifford Reeder, Adrian Willmott, Jamie Turner, Keith Bassett and Patricia Ashton.

Ten years of hard work had finally come to fruition and were to be of great benefit to such an important organisation in the building of character and initiative. It must be remembered that Mr and Mrs G. H. Gratton and Mr and Mrs S. Wooldridge were the donors of the site in Crediton Road on which the Scout hall was erected.

The Okehampton Rotary Club was founded in 1964 but the ladies were not to be left behind and the Okehampton Inner Wheel celebrated their Charter Night with a dinner at the Ockment Café in Fore Street on 19 May 1965.

Mrs Beatrice Fullwood was the Charter President, following in the steps of her husband, Wilfred Fullwood, the popular and respected Okehampton solicitor, who had been the Charter President of the Okehampton Rotary Club.

Back Row: Ann Bassett, Ivy Hancock, Lily Allin. Middle Row: Helen Rae, Gladys Hayhurst, Vera Laws, Marjery Jones, Marjorie Sweet, Margaret Weaver. Front Row: Connie Maddaford, Molly Carter, Beatrice Fullwood (Charter President), Gwenyth Orsler, Jacky Wonnacott, Susie Brock.

The Okehampton & District Lions' Club was formed in March 1974 due mainly to the energy and enthusiasm of the Charter President Eddie Langan. Part of Lions International, it is said to be the largest organisation of its kind in the world!

It was a proud moment when Eddie received the Charter from District Governor Cyril Hardboard, watched by many of the charter members in the appropriately named Charter Hall.

The Okehampton members came from all walks of life, professional, business, highly regarded tradesmen and three much respected policemen. Throughout the years since, Okehampton Lions have continued to provide items for many deserving causes as well as carrying out much good work too numerous to mention. In the picture, from left to right, are: Brian Pinney M.B.E., Ray Vallance, Ron Day, Viv Gammon, Bob Gee, Mike Curtice (obscured), Den Glanville, Mike Phear, Brian Barkwill, Cyril Hardboard (District Governor), Keith Redstone, John Benyon, Jack Kelly, Basil Bevan, Eddie Langan (Charter President), Sam Sheppard, Mike Lavis, Jim Elson, Lloyd Hines.

Okehampton People

The White Hart provided their normal warm welcome and hospitality to the Okehampton Ladies' Putting Club in 1970.

Started in 1935, by tradition the club always invited the Mayoress as the principal guest to the dinner and this year it was the turn of that popular figure, Polly White. In later years she was, of course, elected Mayor and subsequently was deservedly awarded the M.B.E.

All the members contributed much to the life of the town, but Ernestine (Nibs) Morgan had a particular claim to fame, as she was the first lady to obtain a private pilot's licence at the Barnstaple and North Devon Flying Club in 1936, in what was really a male-dominated preserve – Well done Nibs!

Standing: Dorothy Oag, Mrs Edgecumbe, Dorothy Coombe, Mattie Medland, Kay Judge, Gladys Hayhurst, Irene Wooldridge, Ellen Hoare, Doris Healey, Carrie Marsden, Peggy Brooking, Ellen Webb, Nibs Morgan, Margaret Nash. Sitting: Elizabeth Ash, Mary Worden, Beatrice Fullwood (President), Polly White (Mayoress), Rose Stinchcombe and Olive Wyatt.

The Okehampton Golf Club was initially formed on 21 May 1901, wound up in 1904 but

resurrected as the Okehampton Golf Club Ltd. and re-opened in July 1913.

This was at first almost a male preserve but times were changing and this 1950s photograph of Ladies' Day illustrates some of the eminent ladies who contributed much to the golf club.

Back Row: Mrs Weaver, Mrs Burgess, Mrs Giddy, Mrs Phillips, Miss Fulford, Mrs Powell.

Front Row: Mrs Cook, Mrs Wilder, Mrs Fisher, Mrs Westlake, Mrs Cornish, Mrs Holmnes.

Popular businessman Bill Cornish was elected Mayor in 1960, and following the Mayor Choosing Ceremony in the Town Hall, the 'town' was invited to the traditional buffet reception in the Market Hall. Here, Bill and Mavis Cornish are pictured with members of the Borough Council and officers with the 'town silver'. The silver maces were presented to the old Corporation by His Grace the Duke of Bedford on 14 September 1761 and the Grace Cup by Christopher Harris M.P.,whose arms it bears, around 1680.

Left to Right: R. A. Brunskill (Engineer & Surveyor), Rev. Radford (Mayor's Chaplain), J. J. Newcombe (Former Town Clerk), Reg Horne, Bill Brock, Ron Taylor, Eric Rae, Walter H. Passmore, Mavis Cornish (Mayoress), Leslie Martin, Bill Cornish (Mayor), Bill Letchford, Jimmy Laws, Walter J. Passmore, Jim Fogaty (Bank Manager), C. A. Orsler (Town Clerk).

Traditionally, in the evening following his election, the Mayor has held a civic banquet. In 1960, however, Bill Cornish departed from this and, instead, held a 'Young People's' Dance in the Market Hall and pictured are a few of the guests being welcomed by the Mayor and Mayoress.

Standing: Bill Cornish (Mayor), Anthony Steeples, Dilys Jordan, Derek Cauldwell, ? , Terry Acton, Derek Drew, John Day, Horace Rutley, Joan Newcombe, Bill Kelly, ? , Paul Hellyer, William Cornish. Sitting: Mavis Cornish (Mayoress), Pat Collacott, Julia Cornish, Jennifer Bassett.

This fine array of local business and professional men are pictured here as the Okehampton Rotary Club founder members on 5 May 1964 at the Market Hall. As well as contributing so much to the town and area in their normal life, the formation of the Rotary Club enabled them to further their contributions, with many people, charitable and noble causes benefiting from their time and generosity, a fine tradition which is continued by their successors today. It is fitting that the first Rotary President was highly respected Okehampton solicitor, Wilfred Fullwood.

Back Row: J. Laws, C. Bickford, C. Hancock, E. Bassett, R. Hawking. Middle Row: T. Wonnacott, D. Allin, O. Maddaford, Dr Jones, F. Hayhurst, C. Orsler, L. Sweet, L. Weaver. Seated: R. Burgess, J. Singer, Rev. Radford, W. Brock, W. Fullwood (President), C. Carter, R. Parker, E. Rae.

Heavy rain on Wednesday, 10 August 1960 did not deter the large crowd of walkers at the start of the 'Beating of the Bounds' at Okehampton. This was during the Mayoralty of William (Bill) Cornish. It is interesting, however, to note the number of young people attracted to this event.

Among the characters present is bowler-hatted veteran Charlie Sprague who, throughout his lifetime, was ever present at this event.

Mrs Landick's Class of 1925 pose for the camera outside the Victorian School in North Street. The school was almost unchanged from when it was erected in 1877 at a cost of £1,670, initially for girls and infants only, for a total of 400 children.

Two further class-rooms were, however, added in 1896/98 at a cost of £800, and in 1913 several much needed improvements were made, again at a cost of £800.

Mrs Landick was a very popular and hardworking teacher who had the respect of all her pupils, whilst Miss Waghorn was the estimable headmistress. Teaching was in the family blood and her sister taught at the Okehampton Grammar School.

At the time the North Street School, like East Street School (boys only) and the Fowley Down School (mixed) were known as 'public elementary schools' and were all controlled by one set of managers, with the long-serving Charles Sprague of 4 Station Road, as the 'correspondent'.

Back Row: Gwen Cockwill, Nora Walmsley, Edie Vernon, Florrie Drew, May Letchford. 3rd Row: Irene Stoneman, Lily Hain, Barbara Newcombe, Edna Northam, Lulu Woolley, Nancy Drew, Unice Harris, Betty Wykes, Olive Pike. 2nd Row: Phyllis Hill, Florrie Evans, Edna Phear, May Southcombe, Betty Day, Betty Jury, Rose Bullin, Enid Sleeman. Front: Vera Venton, Winnie Palmer, Dora Colwill, Lily Hunt, Mrs Landick (Teacher), Nancy Smale, Hetty Bevan, Lily Bevan, Ella Bulley.

The reception class of the Okehampton County Primary School for 1992 experienced very different conditions to the children of 1925, as they began their education at the new school at the Showfield site under popular teacher Gillian Lower.

At the official opening, Michael Fallon M.P., Under Secretary of State for Education, described the school as "The best school I have seen since I have been in office".

For the 500 or so pupils who attend the school, it is certainly an improvement on the ramshackle Victorian building which had been used for so many years. Back Row: Amy Stephens, Ben Denham, Lena Haydon, Matthew Harvey, Jody Leahy, Jonathon Miller, George Hammond. 3rd Row: Scott Ditchburn, Holly Pickstock, Kirsty Newberry, Gary Langan, Heather Smith, Robbie Hatten, Hayley Morris, Philip Evans. Seated: Kerrie Drew, Martyn Partridge, Christopher Godbeer, Rhea Murrin, Gillian Lower (Teacher), Melanie Vanstone, Ricky

Moore, Timothy Hood, Michael Daddo. Front Row: Hannah Stevens, Katherine Lunk, Kirsty Abbott.

One of the many attributes of the Congregational Church in North Street was the strength of the junior church. The church offered a varied menu of activities and entertainment to contribute to the normal spiritual and moral well-being of the children, as this 1956 drama production illustrates. The cast of 26 were well supported by back-stage and front-of-house helpers, the hours of rehearsal paying dividends in faultless performances, with many proud parents in the audiences.

Standing: Ron Hayhurst, Muriel Evans, Jenny Lee, Joan Thompson, Eileen Kelly, Alistair Macbeth, Pat Dawkins, Graham Hoare, Christine Bubear, John Arthur, Olive Dowden, Josie Marles, Diane Worden, Tony Walmesley, Phyllis Dyment, Jean Ellis, Hilary Bird, Jean Marles, Pauline Day, Kenny Hatten. Sitting: Frank Chammings, David Chammings, Alan Furse, Michael Evans, Tony Connor, Alan Hatten.

The senior scholars of the Okehampton Primary School distinguished themselves on 22 June 1950 by giving what was described in the press as "One of the best juvenile performances seen in the town for years". The children contributed 'Peach Blossom', an operetta by L. Ramsey, where they recaptured in colourful and tuneful style the spirit of old Japan. The costumes were made by parents and teachers and many pupils were able to benefit from the physical training equipment purchased from school funds boosted by the proceeds from the performance.

Back row: Bernard Middleton, Peter Bray, Leslie Vernon, Valerie Baker, Davina McKenzie, Neville MacKay, Paul Voaden, John Wayborn, Joan Pauley (Teacher and Producer). Middle row: Roger Slee, Trevor Hutchings, Barry Grant, Bobby Green, Jean Westlake, Robert Gill, Jean Lee, Gerald Bird, Michael Sanders, Bobby Ware. Front row: Alan Gaywood, John Hannaford, Trevor Collins, Jimmy Little, Michael Evans, John Holland, Erica Barnes, Marion Cockwill, Eileen Kelly, Rosemary Nash, June Harnell.

In 1943, Okehampton bandsmen, reinforced by servicemen home on leave, head a church parade for American soldiers in Market Street. Those shown include: H. Sampson, J. Bulley, W. Holding, B. Pellow, R. Stoneman, Audrey Friend, and L. Walters.

Gales' Premier Dance Band pause for the camera during the ball at the Drill Hall in 1937 to raise funds for the Okehampton & District War Memorial Hospital. This was in the days prior to the National Health Service, with the hospital being self-supporting. The band members always volunteered their services free for this worthy cause.

Always immaculately dressed, this picture of the accomplished musicians will evoke many fond memories from either side of the war.

During the war years, conductor Jimmy Gale, with restricted band members, certainly kept the 'home fires burning' as the servicemen of many countries stationed in the area danced to his music. Sadly, however, Cyril Bevan was killed in action.

This popular Okehampton Band finally called it a day in 1960, but their music will not be forgotten. Left to right: Henry Weeks (trumpet), Cyril Bevan (string bass), Arthur Bevan (trumpet and guitar), Bob Gale (tenor sax), Betty Gale (drums and sax), Les Gale (alto sax and clarinet), Jimmy Gale (accordion and piano).

War clouds are looming and the Okehampton Borough Band, under bandmaster Ogden, are seen outside the Market Hall premises.

It is a little known fact that the Borough Band was financially supported by the town council and the bandmaster was paid a salary.

Back Row: Bill Bird, Skip Rogers, Harry Metters, George Bird, Harold Bevan, Ben Luxton, Arthur Taylor, ? . Middle Row: Jack Smale, Archie King, Les Walters, ? , Jim Bulley, Jimmy Crocker. Front Row: Reg Maddaford, Dick Mills, John Yolland, Wally Holden, Bandmaster Ogden, Tommy Bevan, Bill Crocker, George Bird Snr., Nathan Carter.

There was great rivalry between the two bands in Okehampton and, like the Borough Band, the Okehampton Excelsior Silver Band of 1937 boasted many accomplished musicians, none more so than legendary bandmaster Jimmy Gale, who loved his music and seemed to play every instrument with consumate ease!

3rd Row: J. Tancock, H. Weeks, Alan Balment, Arthur Bevan, Reg Hutchings, Balment Jnr. 2nd Row: Roy Weeks, George Glover, Harry Northam, Harold Sampson, Mr Smeardon, Jack Bolt, Sandy Ball. Front Row: Hector Woodley, Bert Pellow, Bob Gale, Jimmy Gale (Bandmaster), Bill Glover, Arthur Vanstone, Bob Gill.

Following nationalisation in 1949, the South Western Electricity Board Branch at Okehampton embarked on a major programme of rural electrification under the SWEB Rural Development Scheme. The total staff based at Okehampton at one time totalled 90.

Over the next 10 to 15 years, whole villages such as Meeth, Patchacott, Spreyton, Inwardleigh, Iddesleigh, Germansweek, Broadwoodkelly, Bondleigh, Monkokehampton as well as numerous others, hamlets and isolated farms and cottages were connected to the mains electricity supply.

Under branch manager C. E. W. (Clem) White, the staff took great pride in their achievement and this 1949 photograph shows a typical construction gang pausing for a well-earned break before completing the erection of an 'H' pole and 11-thousand-volt transformer at Bogtown, Northlew. Left to Right: Jimmy Vanstone, Harold Metherell, Bill Brock, 'Georgie' Mouat, 'Stevie' Stephenson, Horace Lee, Jim Cockwill, Sid (Brummie) Llewellyn, Tom Lake, Arthur Newcombe, Charlie Eggleton.

Below, popular Mayor C. E. W. (Clem) White presents the cup at the March fair in 1961. March fair was traditionally held on the second Tuesday after 11 March and, as can be seen, attracted many respected local farmers as well as dealers from far and wide. No doubt there would be some celebrations in the hostelries once the buying and selling had been completed.

The 26 March 1974 was the last council meeting of the Okehampton Rural District Council as, with local government reorganisation, this was to become part of the now West Devon Borough Council, who still use the premises today. Such was their popularity that many represented their parish for many years and their council experience was one of their many attributes. Many local worthies are recorded in this picture, people who loved the area, and they represented, and fiercely protected, their parishes without any fear of the party politics which are sadly part of local government today. The council consisted of 27 parishes with 33 elected members and a dedicated staff.

Back Row: (staff) Miss Westlake, Miss Jennifer James, Mrs B. Friendship, Ian Cann, J. Gay, E. Tidball, P. Verner, P. Evison, T. Marshall (Deputy Clerk), T. Porter, Miss J. Rice, Miss D. Scantlebury, Miss E. Arscott. Centre Row: L. G. Bailey (Engineer & Surveyor), F. H. Fishleigh (Monkokehampton), J. Sampson (Drewsteignton), J. Darch (South Tawton), Major W. Kettle M.C. (Exbourne), G. Parsons (Okehampton Hamlets), F. Baker (Northlew), J. Hore (Hatherleigh), J. Avery (North Tawton), P. Adams (Northlew), J. Hill (Beaworthy), F. Gerrard (Spreyton), C. Petherick (Meeth), J. Hodge (Okehampton Hamlets). Front Row: T. W. Endacott (Throwleigh), A. J. Knapman (Drewsteignton), Dr Mary Budding (Medical Officer of Health), C. T. Able (Bratton Clovelly), Mrs M. M. Hampson (North Tawton), S. P. Perkin (Germansweek), P. Cleverdon (Hatherleigh), P. Hill (Chagford), J. Knapman (Clerk to the Council), Mrs P. A. Fletcher (Chagford), J. I. Reddaway (Sampford Courtenay), F. C. Western (Broadwoodkelly), F. Dennis (Sourton).

The Okehampton Borough Council had been created by the Charter of 1885 and successive Councils and Councillors had always served the Borough well and, like the Rural, without any Party Political allegiance or thought of expenses. The 31 March 1974 saw the end of the Borough Council and the ensuing photograph, taken outside the Town Hall, will be part of the history of the town forever.

Standing: Harold Bevan (Mace Bearer), Jeff Cunliffe, Richard Elliot, Derek Allin, Joan Pauley, Polly White, Norman Weston, Peter Woodgate, David Middleton, Harry Matthews, Bill Letchford, Harry Smith (Mace Bearer). Sitting: Margaret Nash, Ron Taylor, Clem White, Arthur Dear (Town Clerk), Walter Passmore (Mayor), Reg Horne, Jim Crocker, Dr Jones, T. Bennett.

OKEHAMPTON LIBERAL PARTY.

The Honourable George Lambert represented Okehampton as Member of Parliament, like his father before him, for many years. A gentleman at all times, he enjoyed a large personal vote, which always gave him a substantial majority as a National Liberal and Conservative.

In this picture of the 1950s election he chats with his normal good humour with tellers and supporters of all parties outside the polling station at the Primary School in North Street, having a particular banter with strong Labour Supporter, Norah Gee.

Fred Dennis, much later in life, was to become chairman of the West Devon Borough Council, an honour he thoroughly deserved and which he filled with distinction whilst avoiding party political influences.

'Ginger' Hawkins was, of course, one of the great 'characters' of Okehampton, a cattle drover turned successful cattle dealer and, later, hard-working Councillor and Alderman, but he died before he could fulfil his mayoral ambition.

From the traffic, it can be seen that this was before North Street was designated 'One-Way'. Left to Right: The Hon. Mrs Lambert, The Hon. George Lambert, Mary Hawkins, Miss Miller, Vic Lancaster, Norah Gee, 'Ginger' Hawkins, Major D. P. K. Ryan, Fred Dennis, George Farley.

The Okehampton Liberal Association Children's Party of the 1950s could hardly be described as 'political' as a large number of young people from all sections of the town attended.

The compère is the unmistakable figure of Welshman Trefor Williams, whose laughter and ready smile, whether at work or play, has made him such a lovable character.

In 1947 Westcountry locomotive No. 21c113 was named 'Okehampton'. Built at Brighton, it was the Pride of the Southern Railway. In 1969, it was taken out of service, and British Rail presented the nameplate to the Town Council in April of that year. This photograph, taken in the Town Hall, showed four other councillors who, besides Ron Taylor, would serve or had served the Borough loyally as Mayor.
Left to Right: ? , Bill Cornish, Dr C. G. Jones, British Rail Manager, Mr Willis (Asst. to Town Clerk), Reg Horne, Ron Taylor (Mayor), Clem White, Jimmy Crocker, C. A. Orsler (Town Clerk).

In a distinguished civic life, Walter and Daisy Passmore have attended many important and enjoyable functions.

Although they do their best to raise a smile for the camera, nothing could have been so dispiriting for them as that day in 1972 when Okehampton Railway Station formally closed and "The last train left Okehampton for Exeter St. Davids". Alas, Dr Beeching and the motor car had won the day.

One important side effect was, of course, the dramatic reduction in employment prospects, as so many people in Okehampton and District had found employment in the railway industry.

And the band played! It is Saturday, 24 May 1997 and the Okehampton Railway Station officially re-opens after lying unused and derelict for 25 years.

The occasion was indeed splendid and marked by the Ocean Liner Express, comprising coaches from the Orient Express and Ocean Liner, travelling from Exeter with some 170 official guests.

There was a warm welcome at the station, refurbished at a cost of £750,000.

With cameras snapping at every opportunity, we have produced just one photograph which we feel illustrates the true splendour of the day and the station, which is now open to the public on Sundays throughout the summer.

Congratulations to everyone – this is a credit to the public and private sector partnership which made it all happen.

Congratulations! The award winning Okehampton/Folly Gate Home Guard detachment with yet another Trophy. Some of these excellent members had originally been in the Local Defence Volunteers.

Back Row: 2nd Lt. Reg Lennox-Jones, ?, Stanley Stanbury, Cpl. Jimmy Reddaway, ?, Sgt. George Whieldon.

Sitting: Henry Hooper, Vince Rees, Cpl. Frank Yeo.

Okehampton has provided a cattle market that every farmer wanted and had done so since the Devonshire Domesday, when Okehampton was one of only three Markets mentioned.

This 1950s photograph is typical of a Saturday market, with the unmistakable figure of Vic Savage (with cap, in foreground) deep in conversation with John Dufty.

Vic, as the south-western representative of Walter Gregory of Wellington, was well known in the farming community, with his specialist knowledge of veterinary products. He also played a full part in civic affairs, being elected Mayor of Okehampton in 1983 and 1984.

It was a case of ladies first, however, as his wife, Brenda, had been Mayor in 1980 and 1981.

Sadly these Saturdays will no longer be repeated with the closure of the market, once the life blood of Okehampton – Saturdays will never be the same!

The Girl Guides, Girls' Life Brigade and Red Cross are marching with military precision as they approach Lodge Bridge in the 1959 Mayoral parade.

Amongst those in the foreground are Beryl Rowlands, Jennifer Northam, Jennifer Lowe, Janet Brewer, Pat Goodanew, Ann Lee, Paddy Collacott, Trixie Spencer, Margaret Angel, Eileen Angel, Hilary Bird, June Harris, Anita Luxton, Ann Blatchford, Pauline Jewell, Elizabeth Passmore, Bronwyn Symons and Caroline Hellyer.

Notice the old market buildings which are long since gone.

A rare picture of the combined strength of the Okehampton Boys' Brigade and the Girls' Life Brigade taken in North Street in 1925.

The unmistakable figure of Bob Furse is in the centre with highly-respected Boys' Brigade Captain and businessman Edward Stinchcombe on his left. Edward Stinchcombe did so much good work for the Youth of the Town, and at his funeral service the large attendance testified to the great respect in which he was held. The Rev. Herbert-Jones who conducted the service concluded with "Edward Stinchcombe has crossed the bar and the trumpets sound on the other side". The reason for this 'get together' is the large Exeter and Devon Shield which had just been won, with the two Individual Cups.

Other people included are: Bill Crocker, Alby Newcombe, Cyril Down, Len Jordan, Sam Wreford, Jimmy Crocker, Orville Maddaford, Ken Bubear, Horace Lee, Bill Pike, John Mills, Tim Symons, William (Blimey) Allen, Mr Ridge, Mr Chammings, Winnie Lee, Betty Evely, Edie Dymont, Mary Howard, Vera Vanstone, Bessie Rogers, Beatrice Sillifant and Peggy Stinchcombe (Brooking).

The Okehampton Life Boys assemble in North Street in February 1952 prior to the wedding of one of their officers, Mary Howard, who wed bank clerk Ivor Ganton. The Life Boys, often described as the Junior Boys' Brigade, played an important part in the development of the youth of the town and is an organisation sorely missed.

Left to Right: Captain William Macbeth, Leader Beatrice Sillifant, Peter Henwood, Bob Green, Reg Horne, Kenneth Chowings, Alan Hatten, David Chammings, Barry Smale, Alan Furse, Tony Lowe, Peter Lee, John Westlake, Michael King, Peter King, John Arthurs, Lieutenant Walter Passmore.

One of the light-hearted features of the Okehampton Grammar School year was the annual staff versus school hockey match. This 1935 staff side look in very good spirits as they prepare for the match. Alan Ferriday, who wrote many textbooks, was an outstanding games player, as well as Harry Wackett, who played cricket and soccer at a high standard. Dr E. D. Allen-Price was the school medical officer and medical officer of health for this area.
Back: Alan Ferriday, Geoff Cook, Appleby (sixth-former), Miss Bourne, Miss Powell, Harry Wackett, Miss Lord, Miss Smith. Front: Dr Allen-Price, Mr Morgan, Miss Martin.

The unveiling of the War Memorial Board at the Grammar School was carried out by former Headmaster William Hunter with Deputy Head 'Hoot' Grant. Harry Mills had succeeded Mr Hunter as headmaster but, as a mark of respect, asked his predecessor to carry out this ceremony as he had taught all the fallen. The Grammar School throughout its history had four distinguished headmasters in Hunter, Mills, Ron Felton and Bob Ray and it was the latter who masterminded the change to comprehensive. It is a tribute to their dedication and discipline that the Grammar School enjoyed such a fine reputation and produced so many outstanding pupils.

The Infant children at Okehampton County Primary School always looked forward to the Christmas visit to the Castle Hospital.

Here, in 1960, Father Christmas (Fred Wooldridge), the children bearing gifts, are being supervised by Mrs Down, Mrs King, Grace Gay and Lilian Hosgood. Note there is only a footbridge over the West Okement and the Okehampton Castle Laundry was still a thriving business.

Valentine's Day, 14 February 1971, saw the Okehampton Section of the Dartmoor Rescue Group (D.R.G.) at Cranmere Pool on a celebratory training exercise.

Fred Barlow, the field controller, had recently been appointed to the Mountain Rescue Committee of the UK and had made representations for a suitable stretcher. As a result, the D.R.G. had been issued with one of the Scottish 'Amos McInnes' purpose-made lightweight stretchers, which is seen resting on the famous Postbox. The picture below includes:

'Larry' Fraser, Penny Fraser, Bruce Fraser, John 'Charlie' Pellow, Christine Fraser, 'Mickey' Ireland, Les Forsdyke, Pat Butler, Fred Barlow (field controller), David Jones, a visitor, Paul Barlow, Ian Boyce, Pauline Boyce, Jim Hannaford, Ernie Bassett (base controller).

This 1974 revue by the Okehampton Courtenay Arts Club was described as a 'Happy pick-me-up for the present economic and industrial malaise' by that splendid newspaper the *Western Times*.

Sadly, electricity restrictions limited the show to just two nights but there were no inhibitions from the popular company, as, in their inimitable style, they played their programme of fast-moving sketches, songs, monologues, carols and rousing choruses. Half the profits went to the Dartmoor Rescue Group, which, the programme revealed, has carried out 52 moorland rescues in the 1969–1974 period.

Standing: Dot Matthew, Roger Partridge, Rosina Young, Norman Judge, Joyce Penelly, Larry Ainslie, Derek Adams, Debbie Young, Mary Dunn, Elizabeth Dutton, John Crosbie, Maud Hall, Adrian Thomas. Kneeling: Lily Allin, Ray Vallance. Sitting: Hilary Wreford, Ann Winn-Holland, Alison Vallance.

The 'League of Friends' was formed in 1964 "to provide extra comforts and equipment for the two local hospitals" and over the years, with the considerable help of the people of Okehampton and District, many thousands have been raised to provide equipment which the Health Service have been unable so to do. Here, in 1969, Chairman of the League Clem White officially hands over an electrocardiograph to the Hospital.

Left to Right: Joan Pauley, Peggy Brooking, Norman Judge, Matron Deeks, Clem White, Dr Jowett, Mrs Campbell, Dr Twining, Neville Sampson, Nibs Morgan, Janet Twining.

Okehampton Argyle Football Club were Joint Junior I Winners with Exmouth Amateurs in 1961/62. This team included some fine individual players, with John Wright being a prolific goal scorer over many seasons with the club. This was before the days of the substitutes and only eleven players constituted the team, as you will see from the photograph.

Back Row: D. Hewitt, T. Hutchings, D. Webb, T. Drew, R. Drew, S. Drew. Front Row: M. Webb, T. Hooper, J. Wright, A. Bowden, D. Joslin.

Skipper Trevor Drew, in a long playing career within the club, set a high standard in sportsmanship and was never sent off, booked or even spoken to by the Referee. He now continues his good work as an officer of the club and is still a credit to the game.

The Football Club dinner in the Pretoria on 19 July 1961 included numerous players and officials who served the team for so many years both on and off the field.

So many faces are instantly recognisable that it is hardly necessary to list the names, but nevertheless, we do:

Back Row: David Evans, John Westlake, Michael Webb, Peter Evans, Bob Gee, Trevor Hutchings, Gerald Bird, John Kennard, Trevor Drew, Mike Wreford, John Hill, Bob Westlake, George Madge, Eric Furse, Arthur Bevan, Ron Taylor, Harry Wright, Claude Cockwill. Middle Row: John King, Sid Saunders, Nelson Trewin, Graham Smith, Alan Vernon, Rodney Drew, John Marles, John Wright. Front Row: J. Barker, Jock Walker, Sid Drew, Kenny Drew, Paul Hellier, Trevor Middleton.

Eric Furse was, of course, an excellent player, starting for the town when still at the Grammar School and playing for over 40 years, including skippering the side in their glory years.

George Stillings (Stil) was a much-respected *Express & Echo* journalist and talented cartoonist whose work was featured in that newspaper and in the *Football Express*.

He had a great love of sport and we are delighted, with the permission of the *Express & Echo*, to reproduce two of his works in this book.

The first is of the Okehampton Miniature Rifle Club dinner in 1935, which 'Stil' attended, and his 'impressions' of the distinguished officers of the club at the time are extremely accurate.

Okehampton has always been justifiably proud of its marksmen and it was at the 1949 Annual Dinner that the then Mayor, Alderman W. H. Passmore, said "Rifle shooting possibly demanded more individual skill than most other diversions. If a shot missed the bull, there was an end to it. No one could cover up the mistake. The activity called for particular gifts of steadiness, nerve and a desire to do one's best. As far as Okehampton is concerned, this club is playing its part not only within our own confines but throughout the county, to preserve the social and cultural lives of both. Clubs of this kind do an enormous amount of good in training eyes and nerves and developing patience and a high quality of sportsmanship."

This caused some discussion at the time, as there was some feeling that shooting was an 'Art' rather than a 'Skill'.

Certainly, the sentiments expressed by Mr Passmore are still accurate today, as the Club continues its fine tradition.

'Stil' was always careful to date every cartoon and to identify his subject matter correctly, which is a great help in accuracy for anyone researching the past.

The second inpression was of the Okehampton Bowling Club of 1934, with a rare mistake, when it should, of course, have been Mr G. U. Fulford and not G. V. Fulford as Vice-President. There were certainly some local worthies here, with the redoubtable J. J. Newcombe as President, and perhaps it would be interesting if readers could identify the Members who had served or would serve the Borough as Mayor?

It was interesting that, at the time, the annual subscription was still 2/6d (12$\frac{1}{2}$p) and it remained at this for 25 years, in the period from 1922 to 1947, until it was increased to 5/- (25p), surely a sign of the lack of inflation in those days!

The Club owed much to the 'characters' illustrated above, to their efforts on and off the 'green'.

However, it was Okehampton's greatest benefactor Sidney Simmons who provided a gift of £800 in 1920, a large sum in those days, to make it all happen. This also enabled a considerable number of the unemployed at the time to find work.

In 1922, when it was opened, the 'Simmons Bowling Club' was formed with Sidney Simmons as its first president and patron. Okehampton is indebted a great deal to Sidney Simmons.

This photograph is of the all-conquering Okehampton Rugby Football 1st XV Season 1951/52, during which they played 28 games, 26 of which were won with 2 drawn, as part of a sequence of 34 unbeaten games extending into Season 1952/53. The club then played in Simmons Park, subject to the park keeper's consent. If the ground was declared unfit, the players would take up the posts and re-erect them in a field (now part of the Exeter Road Industrial Estate), taking the posts back to the park for the following week. It was not unusual for the players to be still marking out the pitch just before kick-off time. Turner, Balsdon and Hawkins were county players, whilst Hawkins and Balsdon played for Exeter 1st Team when they were a very strong side.

Standing (L to R): A. Welham (Team Secretary), O. Parker (Secretary), A. Studdon (Treasurer), M. Palmer, W. Fanning, R. Balsdon, E. Hawkins, A. Vanstone, J. Hayes, R. Furze (Committee), J. Cornish (Committee). Seated: G. Stewart, G. Westaway, L. Turner (Captain), D. Brown (President), H. Westlake, P. Moore, S. Head. Front Row: V. Lancaster, T. Cann, T. Coombe.

It is a great pity that the Rugby Side of 1951/52 could not have played against this club team of 1996/97, one of the best seasons ever in the proud history of the club, with the First Team becoming Western Counties Champions and the 2nd XV winning the Devon Merit Table. In addition, the club enjoyed an excellent run in the Devon Cup, knocking out Plymouth Albion on the way and narrowly losing to Barnstaple, played at Okehampton. One thing the 1951/52 side would have admired during their playing days, however, is the magnificent facilities and atmosphere engendered at the Showfield – a credit to the town.

Standing: K. Pollard (Coach), B. Blatchford (Coach), C. Ewen, M. Sansom, I. Thomas, S. Francis, S. Collier, G. Vick, P. Davey, R. Appleyard, A. Searle, K. Lee, D. Mugliston, G. Sage, R. Burgoyne, I. Langbridge, A. Curtis. Seated: P. Balsom (Treasurer), A. Dennis, T. Cann (Secretary), R. Barkwell, E. Pengelly (President), M. Curtis (Captain), D. Curtis (Chairman), D. Bickle, I. Hodge (Chairman of Selectors), S. Penna, N. Folland, R. Westlake (Coach).

The girls' netball side enjoyed similar success to the boys in 1949. Pictured with this team is headmaster Reggie Burgess, who, besides setting high standards of discipline and academic achievement, loved sport. He himself represented four counties at rugby as well as playing for the Barbarians. He had five county sportsmen and women on his staff as well as many others of all-round ability, producing players for the local teams.

Standing: Enid Darch, Betty Hawkins, Marie Kelly, Margaret Chastey. Seated: Pauline Fone, Pauline Younger (Teacher), Jill Bicknell, Reggie Burgess (Headmaster), Pat Welham.

The outstanding all-round sportsmen in this football team produced an unbeaten season in 1949. Trevor Drew, as an example, was head boy as well as skippering the soccer, rugby and cricket teams and, in storybook style, scored a century on his first appearance for the school cricket team. Eddie Hawkins held nine of the eleven school athletic records and went on to play rugby for Birkenhead Park, the Army, Exeter and Devon.

Gerald Parsons was an outstanding cricketer and was captain of the Cornwall county side. The school were lucky to have Denzil Mortimer as their soccer coach. He was due to sign for the Arsenal Team but the outbreak of the war precluded what, no doubt, would have been a successful football career. After the war, he returned to teaching at Okehampton, later becoming Headmaster at North Tawton Secondary Modern School before becoming deputy head at Okehampton College, when five schools were amalgamated. His electrifying pace and cannonball shot which

produced so many goals for Okehampton Argyle will always be remembered.

Back row: Eddie Hawkins, Terry Barkwill, Alec Davey, Maurice Martin, Gerald Parsons, Pat Moore, Denzil Mortimer (Teacher). Sitting: Stuart Shobbrook, Oakley Medland, Trevor Drew, Colin Barkwill, Robin Richards. Front Row: Colin Tancock, Eddie Moriarty.

The Okehampton Badminton Club at one time boasted nearly 50 members and often fielded three mixed double sides on the same night.

This 1971 line-up illustrates the support the club had and includes: Cynthia Sheppard, John Medland, Eric Chowings, Kay Hadaway, Phyllis McGaul, Joy Vaughan, Jill Hallett and Iris Bostock, Hilary Wreford, Gordon Vaughan, Brenda Bessell and Brian Williamson.

The Okehampton Argyle colts football team in 1948/49 improved on their success of the previous season by enjoying the cup and league double and are pictured with their cup-winning side outside the Simmons Park Pavilion. The Okehampton and District Minor League certainly developed and encouraged young players and, coupled with the support of the schools, many excellent soccer players were produced.

Back Row: Reggie Beardon, John Hawkins, Eddie Hawkins (Goalkeeper), Maurice Martin, Mike Wreford, Stan Cousins. Front Row: Tim Sanders, Frank Leach, Trevor Drew (Captain), Norman Bevan, Derek Hallett.

Pictured in front of the old wooden pavilion, which was synonymous with Okehampton Cricket Club, are the 1955 stalwarts, who all served the club so well. Tommy Seldon was the deputy head of the Okehampton Secondary Modern School for many years and Reg Kennard was the popular long-serving secretary.

David Tucker skippered the Okehampton club for countless seasons and, but for his farming commitments, would have been an integral part of the county side. Back Row: Thomas Seldon (Umpire), Ken Marsh, A. W. Roberts, Cyril Short, Ken Hayhurst, Ken Westcott, Vic Lancaster, Reg Kennard (Secretary). Front Row: Norman Bevan, David Tucker, Fred Duffy, Harold Martin, David Hearn.

The 1972/73 Season was a successful one for the Columbines and this featured the Okehampton side in February 1973 just before they defeated Torquay 5-3 in a fast flowing game, the combination of the experienced players and the enthusiasm of the younger element proving superior on the day. Standing: Daisy Passmore, Hilary Wreford, Margaret Stoneman, Marie Roberts (Captain), Dawn Pethick, Pat Cann, Jenny White. Kneeling: Carol Skrzpczak, Janet Harris, Diana Rendle, Catherine Woolley, Mary Guy.

The Carnival Queen's float in the 1967 procession was beautifully decorated in royal blue and silver. The Queen, Jean Ainsley, was at her most regal and with her are: crown bearer, Bernard Gay; sword bearer, David Passmore; attendants Liz Carr, Rita Hancock, Rosemary Alford, Helen Cann.

A much-supported fund-raising annual function was the 'Squires' Charity Supper held in the North Street schoolroom (now the library).

In this event, held on 22 December 1956, everyone played their part, with Harold Brooking as the Squire, Joan Pauley as the Squire's daughter, Graham Hoare as the Squire's son and the Vicar, Alfred Tenby.

Two other highly respected figures in Okehampton were certainly typecast, as local G.P. Dr Jones was the Squire's doctor and Wilfred Fullwood indeed the Squire's solicitor.

The Squires Suppers continued for many years, with a fine tradition of amusing speeches and sparkling wit. Graham Hoare was to progress to a fine academic career and, as a coincidence, this was his 21st birthday.

Left to Right: Archie Smale, Walter Passmore, Fred Hayhurst, Joan Pauley, Dr Jones, Mrs Gentry, Wilfred Fullwood, Graham Hoare, Alfred Tenby, Harold Brooking.

The title of this book is a co_____ _ _ what it's all about! *Okehampton People* is a book which features as many of the townsfolk as could be accommodated. Peering from the pages of this social history of the town are a thousand, or more, faces from the town's past and present, from all walks of life. Here we find choirboys and councillors, Baptists, bandsmen and bowlers, Scouts and soccer 'stars', schoolchildren and schoolteachers, ramblers and rugby players, Rotarians and Round Tablers, golfers and Girl Guides – just some of the many people who have shaped the town's social and sporting life down through the years.

   This pictorial record will be the perfect keepsake of the future, a visual record of the good folk who were active in and around the town throughout the twentieth century.

ISBN: 1 899073 60 4   *Price: £2.99*

The
Tongham
Railway

Peter A. Harding